Something Permanent

Photographs by WALKER EVANS

Poetry by CYNTHIA RYLANT

Harcourt Brace & Company   SAN DIEGO   NEW YORK   LONDON

FOR DAV

Photographs courtesy of the Library of Congress

Library of Congress Cataloging-in-Publication Data
Rylant, Cynthia.
Something permanent/photographs by Walker Evans: poetry by
Cynthia Rylant.—1st ed.
p.   cm.
ISBN 0-15-277090-9
I. Evans, Walker, 1903-1975.   II. Title.
PS3568.Y55S66   1994
811'.54—dc20   93-3861

Special thanks to Anna

Designed by Camilla Filancia
First edition   A B C D E

PRINTED IN SINGAPORE

PHOTOGRAPH

He washed his feet for the picture,
even his knees,
and wondered about that man
who cared enough to want him to sit there
for a photograph
even though he didn't have
nothing good to hold in his hands,
nor even a dog to sit by his chair.
It gave him, briefly,
some sort of feeling
of just being
enough.

BARBERS

What they didn't expect
was how much they would love the place.
They didn't expect to love its
delicious sweet scent,
the deep trust of men,
the softness of that.
The talk was good, sure, and the work
easy compared to farming or mining,
the room always warm.
But whoever thought they'd wake up Sundays
and ache for the place just because they knew
it was heaven
and knew, shamefully,
miserable sinners that they were,
it was more than they deserved.

He told her that if she'd come with him
they could stay at his sister's in Vicksburg
then catch the Greyhound north for Pennsylvania,
and maybe there he'd
find work and they'd make it some way.
She asked how was he going to buy
two bus tickets to Pittsburgh
when he didn't have even a dime, and he said
he'd offer to drive the bus halfway,
and this made some kind of desperate sense to her
so she went.

BOYS

They both loved the same girl
but she wouldn't have either of them
because she was married—
and to the store owner by god,
so it wasn't worth thinking about.
But at night,
they each stretched upon a bed
and had her,
had her whole
and leisurely.
And when they were done,
they settled her back in their minds
like a soft peach
will disappear
into a young boy's pocket,
warm August nights.

SHOES

When he finally died, they kept
them around the house
the longest time,
tripping on them,
arranging them beneath the beds,
occasionally borrowing them
in bad weather.
Then the preacher told them
it was a sacrilege to the dead,
moving those shoes around
like a couple of mop buckets.
So they left them out at the cemetery one day,
and of course the shoes promptly disappeared.
It was impossible for them, after that,
to keep from looking down at the feet of every
person who crossed their path.
And this would have gone on probably forever
had not one of his hats
turned up
way in the back of the closet.

APARTMENT

When her relatives from the south
came up for a visit,
they lamented her sorry state,
having to live in that little box,
having no fields nor trees,
having no hills to look toward.
She never told them
how she didn't miss those things,
how she would lie awake at night,
her apartment window wide open,
and listen to the city
like she was listening to birds,
like she was listening to hymns,
like she was hearing a lover.
She never told them how hard it was
to wipe that smile off her face
each and every minute they complained.

BIRDHOUSES

People said they were
a good excuse
for looking up.

ROCKER

She wanted to be sure to hear the
other babies if they cried,
so she nursed them, one at a time,
at the bottom of the stairs
then carried them,
one at a time,
softly up,
their small
hearts
beating.

He thought it had been a good idea,
giving up the barn to advertisers that way,
but it seemed the more signs that went up,
the sicker his wife got,
'til he counted the days left to her
based on how much entertainment was passing through,
and when the whole building was finally covered,
she took one long look out the window
and died.
After he buried her, he made a small
attempt to strip some of that mess off,
but he couldn't help it,
he liked those damned signs,
so he left them for God to take care of
as He saw fit,
and hoped the Lord wouldn't be too hard on him.
He couldn't help it he'd always been such
a sucker for a show.

BED

Of course it was hard to make love
with the children in the room
but that didn't keep them from trying,
and they were pretty successful,
some would say,
since they had seven kids now.
He would begin it by reaching over
and softly pulling at a slender piece of
her long hair,
wrapping it in his fingers,
and then,
dead tired but still in love,
they would turn toward each other and,
nestled in the warm breathing
of their other babies,
ease their weary minds
with the sex
they knew would likely make them
poorer
and richer
all the same time.

TRAVELER

He swore to God he'd get out
by sixteen, seventeen at the latest,
and when twenty hit,
and him still there,
it hit hard,
and from then on he carried
this heavy anchor inside
that said
you ain't going nowhere, son,
so just get your ass
on home.

MANTEL

She knew about beauty,
and understood it,
and if she just could have afforded to,
she'd have had her children's faces
on that mantel.
But instead she decorated
with what she had
and wished hard in winter
for summer
and the flowers she'd eventually find
to put there.

TOMBSTONE

There wasn't much excitement to be found
anywhere nearby,
so people would just go to the cemetery
when they wanted to give their
visiting company something interesting to do,
and they'd show them
the man and his dog,
and folks would marvel
and say things like,
how do you s'pose they
got them ribs in that dog,
and
I wonder if the dog's buried, too,
and
how much you figure a tombstone
like this'd cost?
Then, without fail,
before leaving
each had shyly to
lean over and stroke that lovely dog's head,
swallowing back the "good boy"
that was on their wondering lips.

HOUSE

She loved it with all her heart
and on warm days would take a blanket
out into the yard so she
could just sit and look at it.
She never once complained about the
work it took to
keep it clean
nor about being so far from things,
living outside of town.
She loved it.
And when her husband said
he was taking a job in Chicago
and they'd have to be moving,
she was sick on and off for weeks
until it finally occurred to her
that staying sick would keep them there.
She developed the most awful cough,
and now and then a patch of her hair would fall out,
but she never felt so bad
she couldn't do a little dusting.

And he thought that if he could
just get those plants up to the top
of the window he might be able
to smile at his kids,
make love to his wife,
enjoy his coffee,
and sleep.

FILLING STATION

Everybody wanted that job
and when Ferrell Brown's son
got it,
when Mr. Brown's son got to pump gas
and flirt with pretty girls all day long,
they all said it was a crock,
that that boy never worked a day
in his life, never had to,
with his rich daddy,
so how come he got a job that
plenty other decent boys with real
need wanted.
Then word got around about
the boy's mother
and how she was walking through that
house stark naked and
trying to hang dinner plates on the
clothesline,
and people shut up about the
Brown boy.
Real need is a personal thing,
they said.
And his mother's a loon.

MINSTRELS

It didn't matter if nobody remembered them later on.
They'd had a few moments to themselves,
on that stage,
and nobody knew
how much they would have *paid*
to get that time
when no white folks
could interfere
in their lives.
When not a person on this earth
could touch or disturb them,
lest be accused of spoiling what
some considered a good show.
They would have worked for free,
like slaves,
just for those minutes
of being no such thing.

MULE

He loved her,
though he never let on,
and not just because having her
raised him up the social ladder
a notch.
No, because she had a hell of a
sense of humor
and seemed to enjoy his company
more than most.
He knew better than to get attached
to a mule,
because one season of bad crops
and he'd be back to
pushing the plow himself,
selling her for beans and lard and
trying to forget he'd almost
turned her into something permanent.
A friend.

GRAVE

It was customary to decorate
a child's grave with something pretty
from the house
and a china plate
was as pretty as they had,
though it gave them
not one bit of solace,
and they worried
late in the evening
some dog or somebody
had come along
and tipped it over,
making their boy's grave
look a foolish thing
and it wasn't.
It wasn't.

GUNSHOP

He was the most important man in town,
the only seller of firearms in the county,
though he knew if it hadn't been for his
granddaddy's money
he'd be walking north to the coal mines
with every other piece of white trash.
But he was important,
knew it,
and whoever walked through the door was humbled,
having to ask to hold this gun or that one,
having to ask if they might trade him something
since money was tight,
trying to work their way in.
But he didn't need to strike any deals.
He had well over three hundred firearms
and a room full of ammunition
and nothing but fellowship
waiting
at his door.

The newspapers could have been put to
better use, of course,
but everybody agreed that
having that paper on the walls
made the family feel a whole lot better—
and the mosquitoes were all so
damned frustrated,
it was worth it.

He opened it because he loved
being his own boss and because he'd
always liked the solitude of the camera.
Always liked being the only one involved.
Then after maybe a hundred or two hundred
photographs
it came to him that he was snapping
destinies
and that the faces lining his walls
were going to die of whooping cough
or heartbreak
and disappear
and disappoint
and go mad
and it got so
he couldn't look at them
on his way out the door
or he'd be up all night wondering when:
when their careful features
would one day spin out of control.

UTENSILS

And when the children would come in
from working the fields,
their bellies aching with hunger,
the tallest of them would
pull out a few spoons, and,
more silent than children should ever be,
they'd stir some cornbread into milk
and eat.

CHURCH

It wasn't easy being a sinner
with God Himself living right next door,
so most of the tenants
climbed out of bed Sunday morning
and went on over to church,
hoping to shake some of that feeling they'd get
every time they hung their underwear
smack beneath the cross.

STORIES

So what are you gonna do
while you're waiting for
a little work,
'cept find somebody else
who's waiting, too,
and swap some stories.
Hell, story's the only thing that's free in this world.

WASH

Wash day was Wednesday,
everybody knew that,
so here come this woman
out of Louisiana into town
who did hers on Friday
and everybody was fuming
because order is order,
and even coal camp living
has got to have its principles.
And wash day was Wednesday.

CAFE

He'd sneak away from the house
when he could
and ride down for a Coca-Cola
and that delicious smell
of food and company
it seemed he never could get
unless somebody'd died.
And though they knew he
wasn't supposed to be there,
knew his mother had said
he was not to loiter in a public
eating place,
the owners took pity on him
and gave him one of their dark green booths
by the window
and never expected to sell him
more than one Coca-Cola
and a half-hour of, well,
some kind of mercy.

LAND

She thought she could remember a time
when the land was beautiful to her,
and the clouds were the province
of angels,
the trees shelter,
the fields wide open running.
But her back had not stopped hurting
her for decades now
and her fingers always had a sting
and eyes red and tired,
and she figured she must be mistaken,
must have heard something in church
about that,
because the earth never was nothing
but work.

MISSION

Lord it was no place
for a man to end up.
He'd walked circles around it for days.
But when he finally did pass through that door
and feel the preacher's hands
on his tired, warm head,
the shame slipped off him like rain
and he was a child again:
hungry,
still,
pure.

AUTHOR'S NOTE

These photographs were taken in the 1930s, when Walker Evans traveled in search of America. A young man then, Evans had been hired by the Farm Security Administration to document the country during the Great Depression. The photographs that came out of the FSA project, Evans's and others', are some of the finest in the world, and many have become quite famous.

During this period Evans also collaborated with the writer James Agee, documenting the lives of rural tenant families in Alabama. Their work together culminated in the book *Let Us Now Praise Famous Men*, which became a legend in American publishing.

PHOTOGRAPHS

12/94